Manifestation Secrets Demystified

Advanced Law of Attraction Techniques to Manifest Your Dream Reality by Changing Your Self-Image Forever

Law of Attraction Short Reads, Book 6

By Elena G. Rivers

Copyright Elena G. Rivers © 2020

All rights reserved. No part of this publication may be reproduced, stored in a retrieval system, or transmitted, in any form or by any means, electronic, mechanical, photocopying, recording, or otherwise, without the author and the publishers' prior written permission.

The scanning, uploading, and distribution of this book via the Internet or via any other means without the author's permission are illegal and punishable by law. Please purchase only authorized electronic editions and do not participate in or encourage electronic piracy of copyrighted materials.

Elena G. Rivers © Copyright 2020 - All rights reserved.

ISBN: 978-1-80095-062-7

Legal Notice:

This book is copyright protected—it for personal use only.

Disclaimer Notice:

Please note the information contained in this book is for inspirational and entertainment purposes only. Every attempt has been made to provide accurate, up to date, and completely reliable information. No warranties of any kind are expressed or implied. Readers acknowledge that the author is not engaging in the rendering of legal, financial, health, medical, or professional advice. By reading this book, the reader agrees that under no circumstances are we responsible for any losses, direct or indirect, which are incurred as a result of the use of the information contained within this book, including, but not limited to, errors, omissions, or inaccuracies.

The information provided in this book is for entertainment purposes only. If you are struggling with serious problems, including chronic illness, mental instability, or legal issues, please consult with your local registered health care or legal professional as soon as possible. This book is not a substitute for professional or legal advice

Contents

Manifestation Secrets Demystified 1

From the Author – Your Personalized LOA Cookbook 9

The #1 The Most Powerful Manifestation Principle That Took Me Years to Learn (+ the Three Magical Words That Can Instantly Change Your Reality!) 20

The Indisputable Law of Self-Image 30

Secret #1 The Number One Question You Absolutely Can't Ignore 36

Secret #2 Trying to Re-Program Your Subconscious Mind? Discover Why It Might NOT Work Unless You De-Program It First 44

Secret #3 The Missing Links between Desire and Aligned Action (and the Best Manifestation Shortcut) 66

Secret #4 Manifest Faster By Slowing Down! (The #1 Thing to Learn from Mindful Manifestors) 76

Secret #5 Does Your Environment Block Your Manifestations? (Feng Shui It Up to Show the Universe You are Ready to Receive!) 84

Conclusion – Trust Yourself 92

Free LOA Newsletter + Bonus Gift 96

More Books by Elena G. Rivers 98

Introduction

From the Author – Your Personalized LOA Cookbook

"Elena, I don't think you should write this book. It's too generic. You didn't niche down properly. What about designing your reader avatar? I mean, are you writing for men or women? Are your readers already successful with manifestation? Or are they new to it? On a scale from 1-10, how would you rate their success level using Law of Attraction Principles? Honestly, judging from your outline, I don't think you should waste your time writing this book. What if people get confused?".

These were the words of a friend of mine, a very successful digital marketer and sociologist. He just wanted to help me and shared his honest feedback. As a very logical person, all the decisions he takes are based on data and only data.

I certainly don't think he's a naysayer. In fact, he's a very positive person. But, when it comes to marketing, he's pretty set in his ways. And yes, he's very successful with

Introduction

what he does. Following his recipe for success serves him well.

However, there's also intuition and creativity. And this feeling inside your gut telling you to do something.

So, this is how I got the idea to write this book. Even though many people, suggested otherwise.

But, I still decided to write it despite my friend's words that I didn't have enough data to write it correctly.

What does "correct" mean anyway? And why am I starting this book in such a weird way?

It's simple - we are all different, and we all resonate with different things. We can't all think and act the same way, imagine we did, the world would be so dull!

Long-term happiness and abundance are created thanks to balance. It's all about balancing logic and data with intuition and creativity.

At the same time, two people may perceive the same thing differently. For example, my friend thinks that my reader avatar is not clearly defined in terms of

Introduction

demographics: "I mean, Elena, are you writing for men or women? And how old are they?"

At the same time, my heart tells me: *"You can go ahead and write this book Elena, you already know your reader avatar. You write for ambitious souls, that's it. And you also know you don't write for people who expect instant fixes or lottery wins without attempting to add any value to the world."*

So, here I am, writing a book with a slightly different structure than my other books in *the Law of Attraction Short Reads* series. While most of my other books are written as systems and programs with specific steps to follow, this book is more like a creative recipe book with no particular order to follow.

It's a creative recipe book for the mind to help you align with the right manifestation principle for you and your current journey. Take what you like and reject the rest.

Imagine you get a new cookbook with a ton of recipes in it. Even if such a cookbook is related to a diet you particularly enjoy, there's no way you'd like all the recipes it contains. You'd most likely pick a few you think

Introduction

will taste good. Then, you'd keep making them so that you can get better and better.

Would you even try to force yourself to make a recipe you know you won't enjoy, judging from the ingredient list or a preparation method?

Of course not.

Yet, when it comes to manifestation and the Law of Attraction, it seems like so many people desperately try to torture themselves with techniques and exercises they don't even resonate with.

For example, some people, such as myself, are scripting and journaling junkies. And so, it's no wonder that any manifestation methods that involve writing, for example, writing things you're grateful for, work well for them.

When you love what you do, you feel good and raise your vibration. It's as simple as that.

But some people don't like the idea of daily writing and journaling. Perhaps, they would do better with a different manifestation method or a slight variation of it. Perhaps, they can write something only once and stick it to their

Introduction

vision board. Or maybe they'd enjoy affirmations more than writing? Or perhaps daily visualization is what makes them tick?

So, be sure to choose a recipe you like. Don't force yourself into practicing LOA methods you don't enjoy, as that can create stress and resistance.

Stress and resistance lead to contraction and negativity. And to manifest beautiful things into your life, you need to focus on expansion and positivity.

The most important thing to focus on is who you are – your mindset and energy are everything.

Back to our cookbook example: a person can choose a fantastic recipe, but since they are not adequately focused and remain negative, they will make a few mistakes while cooking, therefore spoiling their efforts.

So, it's so important to feel positive and expectant while having fun with the process of "cooking your dream reality." Use this rule for any mental or spiritual exercise you choose to do.

Also, each recipe (or preparation method) requires some time. A more sophisticated dish may even require two

Introduction

hours or more to prepare. And so, a smart cook will have fun in the process, by listening to music or talking to someone. They will not get impatient, or angry with the recipe while complaining: "Why is it taking so long?" Also, an inexperienced cook might need even more time because they will often screw things up and attempt to make the same recipe several times, which is absolutely fine! It's all about learning and practicing.

Yet, when it comes to manifestation, so many people get impatient and cynical. I'm not judging; I used to be one of those impatient souls too! And it was my lack of patience that was blocking my positive manifestations. In fact, I would only manifest things that were making me more frustrated and impatient—such a vicious cycle!

It was when I decided to focus on the "recipes" I enjoyed while mastering them, without mindlessly attempting to speed up the "preparation method" or "cook several recipes" at once, that my manifestation journey took off.

This is my intention for writing this book. I want you to pick 1-3 "recipes" that you feel like your mind will enjoy and commit to them while mindfully declaring that from now on, you are the master of your own reality.

Introduction

If you choose a method you really enjoy, just stick to it. There's no reason to switch things up unless you really feel like it. Listen to your intuition.

But before we dive into our Timeless Manifestation and Law of Attraction Secrets, I'd like to share some of the biggest lessons I've learned on my LOA journey.

It doesn't matter whether you're new to LOA or have already read hundreds of books about it. To create your dream reality successfully, you only need to pick one recipe you will enjoy.

Also, don't get discouraged by the word "Advanced" in the title. From my experience, I can tell you that *advanced* is very often much more straightforward and effective than *beginner*. Why not think of yourself as an Advanced Manifestor already? Why call yourself a beginner? I mean: you've manifested this book!

So, you're an advanced Manifestor and will get awarded with incredible, advanced techniques for you to enjoy!

Yes, I know! Our minds love playing tricks with us: *Oh come on, you're not good enough now, start with something more beginner-friendly!*

Introduction

Well, this may be true in some cases.

But, when it comes to manifestation and the Law of Attraction, it's very often by setting higher goals and dreaming bigger that we can manifest our dream reality using the principles of simplicity and mindful repetition of what works for us.

So, without any further ado, let's get started!

Your Free Gift

Free LOA Newsletter + Bonus Gift

Before we get into our *Manifestation Secrets*, I'd like to offer you a free gift designed to help you raise your vibration while eliminating resistance and negativity.

To sign up for free, visit the link below now:

www.loaforsuccess.com/newsletter

Enjoy!

The #1 The Most Powerful Manifestation Principle That Took Me Years to Learn (+ the 3 Magical Words That Can Instantly Change Your Reality!)

Creating your own reality can be easier than you think – if you just understand its fundamental principle.

I used to believe that what happened in the past happened to me. I thought the past had the power to create my future. Even after I began reading about the Law of Attraction, I still held onto my old belief. I somehow thought that other people deserved more success and happiness, but I didn't.

I was stuck in a job that drained me. Then, I repeated the same negative pattern by chasing different business opportunities. I thought that by changing the vehicle (the way I was earning an income), I would manifest more money and abundance.

The Most Powerful Manifestation Principle

And yes, sometimes you need to change the vehicle – this can be your job or business model. However, the change must come from your authentic desire and passion for a new vehicle. Well, in my case, I was all in fear and desperation. No matter what I did, I couldn't get out of the negative cycle of negativity. I felt so depressed because other people could indeed succeed! They could try a new manifestation method and have success with it.

They could apply for a new job and get it. Or manifest it unexpectedly. They could start a new business venture and be successful. They could invest in coaching or business training. They could just follow the steps outlined in some program and create something incredible.

But I couldn't! Even though I was *doing exactly* what they did. I'm sure you can sympathize with my frustration. I thought something was wrong with me. I thought I was doing this personal development thing all for nothing.

I was learning about LOA, I was setting more intentions, I was trying to stay focused on them, and I was trying to think positive thoughts. But my self-image didn't change. You see, I still thought of myself as an average person. An average employee who works hard for peanuts. Just an average person who attempts a business opportunity from a place of lack and desperation.

So, nothing was changing for me. Yes, every now and then, I could experience a little synchronicity or a small manifestation, such as manifesting a cup of coffee or an unexpected bonus at work.

But instead of being grateful and seeing those little wins as the signs of success, my old, limited self-image saw them as signs of failure.

Look at yourself, Elena...all that time and money you spent on self-development. And what did you get? A cup of coffee and a bonus of $50? Whereas other people can manifest amazing relationships, nice houses, luxury travel, and high-paying jobs or businesses they love.

And, so my self-talk and my self-image would dictate my behaviors while creating my reality.

Then, one day, I hit rock bottom. I experienced an anxiety attack. I just cried and cried and cried. I even decided to get rid of all my self-development books and programs and "move on."

The Most Powerful Manifestation Principle

You see, Elena, you made a fool out of yourself! This stuff is not for you. It works for other people because they are smarter. But it will never work for you.

But then, I caught myself repeating these three words – *work for you, work for you, work for you.*

I immediately stopped crying. I washed my face and looked at myself in the mirror. I could still hear these three words: *work for you, work for you, work for you.*

Then it dawned on me! Yes, it was already working for me, and I was already using the Law of Attraction. The problem was that I wasn't using it to my advantage.

Why? Because of my negative self-image backed up by the negative self-talk. My own limitations and negative beliefs about what was possible for me were blocking most, if not all, positive manifestations from my life.

Suddenly, I felt such a relief. Yes, technically, my life was still a mess. I was still recovering after an abusive relationship and a failed business that drained me.

Yet, I still felt empowered! It was as if all those beautiful and empowering self-development and law of attraction lessons suddenly made sense!

At the same time, I thought: "Hold on....you are very good at this! You can use your self-image to create your reality. The problem is that you've been using it negatively. The good news is that now you really feel and understand that this stuff works, and it can work for you if you change your self-image and decide to stop limiting yourself. "

Work for you, work for you, work for you...

You can use your self-talk and self-image to implant positive images in your mind. You can shift your identity and enjoy your new reality. Don't wait. It's already inside you. Allow it to manifest by changing who you are.

It was a very spiritual moment. And I began crying again, but this time, out of joy!

From then on, I felt like a new person, and my life was profoundly transformed. Even though technically, I was still in debt, had no real friends, and on a meager income, I felt like a different person. I felt successful. I could see

The Most Powerful Manifestation Principle

myself in a different reality, doing what I love for a living, being surrounded by people who love and appreciate me, and having the time and resources to help and inspire other people.

To cut a long story short, this is how my real manifestation journey started. I decided to change my self-image. I saw myself in a different reality and began acting in alignment with my true desires. I stopped acting based on my limitations on what I thought other people wanted me to do. From then on, my life began to change. I shifted my identity and attracted a new reality.

I know you can do the same! And I feel very privileged to be sharing with you exactly what worked.

Remember these three power words: *work for you, work for you, work for you.* Keep repeating them whenever you're feeling stuck because they hold the key to your new self-image and dream reality.

"Your Past Does Not Equal to Future" – Tony Robbins

Mr. Robbins put it brilliantly. I would also add my humble words here: *you can experience your dream* future right here, right now, in the present moment. The question is, what do you want it to look like?

Exercise:

Design a vision for your dream life now and create a short mission statement for each area of your life:

My health

Example:
-*I choose to eat healthy foods that give me unstoppable energy and vibrant health.*

-*I love foods that nourish my body.*

-*I'm blessed to indulge in long baths and beautiful walks in nature.*

My Passion/ Purpose / Fulfillment
Example:

-*I feel so grateful I found my calling in life.*

-*I'm even more grateful I can do my passion for a living.*

-*My purpose sets my soul on fire!*

My relationships

Example:

-I get amazingly well with my family, friends, and the man/woman of my dreams.

-We're all happy people; we love and support each other.

-I attract high vibe people into my life.

Money/finance

Example:

-I'm open to receiving.

-I mindfully create new opportunities and new sources of income.

-Money is energy, and I'm energy; therefore, I attract money into my life.

Spirituality

Example:

-I experience unforgettable spiritual moments in my life.

- I feel loved and cared for by the Universe/God/ Higher Power.

That was the first step. Get back to it to remind yourself what's yet to come and how amazing your life can

The Indisputable Law of Self-Image

In his book *Psycho-Cybernetics*, doctor Maxwell Maltz discusses the psychology of self-image. As a plastic surgeon, he observed that it took on average two weeks for most of his patients, after their surgery was done, for their self-image to change. However, Mr. Maltz also observed that some would still feel and act as they did before the surgery unless their inner self-image changed.

He realized that there's something called the cybernetic mechanism, which means that we all have a set point for the way we see ourselves.

Suppose you see yourself as someone who can make only a certain amount of money a year. In that case, your inner resourcefulness will align with that self-image, therefore blocking true abundance.

So, how do you see yourself? If you have a look at the previous exercise, ask yourself: are you still limiting yourself? Perhaps you can re-write your vision?

The Indisputable Law of Self-Image

My old self-image was: *yes, I would like to become an author, but writing is hard, and who would want to read my work anyway? I'm not a famous guru.*

And so, I could never concentrate on writing and felt stuck. It didn't matter what I learned about writing or publishing because I didn't feel worthy of my desires, and my reality kept reflecting that. I couldn't be consistent with my publications.

But there's also another phenomenon to understand. Some people say they really desire something, and they say how badly they want it while creating the energy of desperation. In other words, they put all their desires on a pedestal.

It wasn't until I read the book *Reality Transurfing* by Vladim Zeland that I discovered the hidden dangers of increased importance, and how it can repel our positive manifestations.

Let's say you are getting ready to go for a date, you get obsessed with thoughts such as: *Oh, what if I get rejected? What if this man/woman doesn't like me? I want them to tell me I'm the best, or I'll feel bad!*

The Indisputable Law of Self-Image

And so, you go on a date, and your energy, the way you talk and act, starts reflecting your self-image. You may try hard to manifest something positive, but you attach so much importance to it that, as a result, you reject it.

The Universe can sense your desperate energy. Or perhaps, you're overconfident and start bragging. Well, you may soon encounter unfavorable circumstances manifest to balance out your energy of increased self-importance.

However, if you create a positive self-image of a person who enjoys meeting new people, is friendly, loves socializing, and is a good listener, your date will go much better. When you start focusing on other people and what you can do for them, your energy is authentic, natural, and magnetic.

How many times did you want something so badly that you actually repelled it?
Negative self-image (such as too much desire, self-importance, or lack of confidence) creates resistance. It only activates the law of repulsion.

It's like chasing a cat....and it keeps running away!

The Indisputable Law of Self-Image

In my case, I kept repelling different business opportunities because I wanted money, but at the same time, I wasn't feeling confident about money. I wanted money and success to prove myself to others. And so I unconsciously kept creating very negative energy.

The more worthy you feel inside yourself, the more magnetic you become, and manifestation becomes almost automatic.

Why do you chase money? Is it to get a sense of security or freedom? Well, you can feel these emotions right here, right now.

Focus on your inner relationships with money, love, abundance, and health- whatever it is you desire. Be that person first!

Instead of chasing things, focus on your relationship with whatever it is you want. Whatever it is you want, it's already inside you.

Finally, understand that the self-image you currently have is like a vehicle serving you on your current mission. And even if it's working for you now, at some point, you will need to let go of it and create a new one.

The Indisputable Law of Self-Image

For example, let's say that now, you intend to manifest a freedom-based business because you want to travel the world. So, you create a self-image of someone who can live a laptop lifestyle, and your number one goal is to experience more travel. You join different digital nomad communities and train your mind to look for work or business opportunities that align with your travel goals.

But, maybe after four years of a non-stop digital nomad lifestyle, you decide to settle down. You enjoyed your travels but now feel like slowing down a bit. You want to buy a house and start a family. You no longer wish to be a digital nomad. Instead, you feel like starting a local business and creating job opportunities for your local community.

It's all about understanding who you truly are, right here and right now. Everything is in constant flow. Our energy and priorities can always change. The mistake that so many people make is that they get stuck in their old self-image and old desires that are no longer authentic. It's all about understanding when to let go of the old and embrace the new.

If you have a big dream that you intend to manifest and feel like something is blocking you, chances are it's your old self-image.

The Indisputable Law of Self-Image

For example, when I was getting started on my writing journey, I got stuck in my old self-image of someone who could not finish what they start and gets burned out quickly. But, I knew I had a mission I wanted to accomplish. I knew I wanted to write to raise the vibration of the planet. And so, in alignment with my mission, I had to let go of my old-self image. Instead, I had to create a self-image of an organized and prolific writer who always finishes what they start. In other words, to fulfill my mission, I had to embrace my inner leadership and responsibility.

What is your old-self image? Is it still helpful? If not, create a new self-image that aligns with your current mission! The following pages will inspire you to unleash your hidden manifestation powers in alignment with your true, authentic desires!

Each secret will help you learn a practical law of attraction or manifestation principle or technique. Some secrets will challenge your way of thinking, feeling, or acting. Stick to the secrets that really resonate with you and start mindfully applying them to watch your life transform as you've always wanted!

Secret#1 The Number One Question You Absolutely Can't Ignore

Before you even commence on your manifestation journey, you need to do a quick energy check. Luckily, no complicated rituals are required. You simply need to ask yourself, from what place are you intending to manifest?

If it's from a place of seeking approval and validation from others, you have some work to do! No, I don't want to scare you or make you feel bad about yourself. You should be glad you are discovering it now before it's too late.

So what exactly am I implying? Well, are you stuck on a hamster wheel? Just chasing, chasing, and chasing? And do you feel worthy of manifesting your desires, even before they appear in your reality?

For example, if your main motivations focus on chasing validation and approval, you will feel stuck, no matter what you manifest. You've probably heard many stories of famous people and celebrities who had it all, money, fame, and relationships with other well-known

Secret #1

individuals. Yet, they still felt unhappy or stuck, often resorting to drugs to ease their inner pain.

Another problem with seeking approval is that you may feel tempted to start manifesting goals that are not even yours, to begin with. I have been there so many times! If you have read more of my books in this series, you probably already know my story. If you didn't then, the quick summary of Elena's story is that she spent years chasing and trying to manifest goals that weren't even hers. It took her years of personal development and spirituality work to dive deeper and understand what was really going on. One of the biggest catalysts on her journey was discovering Vladim Zeland's work and reading his book *Reality Transurfing*. After applying his teachings, Elena fully understood that the number one secret to manifesting is to make sure the goal you want to accomplish is genuinely yours.

OK, enough writing about myself in the third person! And back to the main topic – your authentic manifestation energy.

This concept is so important to understand because it can save you years of mindless chasing while stuck on a hamster wheel.

Another thing to keep in mind is that all the entities around you (when I say "entities," I mean both people and the Universe, or any spiritual beings you choose to believe in) can feel your personal energy. If all your actions and thoughts are driven by the need to get validation from others, the energy you create lacks authentic confidence and conviction. No wonder it's hard to manifest what you want. Those around you can feel your inner motives, and the message they receive is:" *Oh OK, he or she wants to get my approval, but they don't approve themselves and lack confidence.* "

Even if you are not into energy stuff, the "stuck on a hamster wheel" concept can also be explained without diving into energy or spirituality concepts.

Let's say a person wants to manifest a better job with a better salary, only because they want others to praise them. So, they go to job interviews. But, they are so self-absorbed that they aren't even able to clearly communicate their value, so they never do well in job interviews. Even if they somehow get their dream job, they are still in the mindset of "I am not good enough" and find a way to sabotage their success or feel stuck again. Yes, they will get some appreciation and feel good about it. But, whenever achievement stops, they will feel bad about themselves: *OMG, nobody is praising me anymore, I'm probably not good enough or doing something wrong.*

In contrast, a person who embraces their true, authentic self-love and seeks a better job because they are passionate about pursuing a new career or working for a specific company can think and act from a place of laser focus. They already feel good and validated within themselves. So they can use all their mental energy to research the company they want to work for and present their value to potential employers in a way that's easy to understand. They don't stress out about the final outcome because they know that even if they don't get their dream job now, they are already validated. Each attempt to seek professional improvement brings them closer to manifesting their dreams whenever the timing is right.

However, a person who wants to manifest because they seek approval and validation might take any rejection very personally: *"Oh no, now they will not love me! I'm not good enough. I should probably try harder."*

Whereas the right question should be: are you even trying to manifest your own goals? And do you want to achieve them because they are in alignment with who you

Secret #1

really are? Or is it because you want somebody to approve you?

You can be in charge of how people around you and the Universe respond to you. It starts with self-honesty. You can choose to embody the energy of natural confidence and conviction now.

I like to use the term "natural confidence" or "authentic confidence" because trying to be more confident can be tricky as well. We often chase confidence thinking it's something we can demonstrate by trying to speak like an authority or making others follow us.

I used to work with quite a few pretty famous online influencers. And let me tell you this- many of them confided in me that they felt tired of acting on social media. It's like putting on a mask to convey a specific image of artificial confidence. So that their followers on social media can get inspired. But then, what happens behind the scenes? Are they the same people on YouTube or Instagram as they are in real life?

One influencer told me that creating a half an hour video felt very painful for her because she had to keep on a mask, which turned out to be exhausting in the long run.

Secret #1

I advised her to be authentic instead. If you choose to lead and influence people, the best long-term strategy is to connect with them on a deeper level. And how can you connect with someone if you can't even connect with yourself by being honest about who you are?

People like honest and real people. So, natural and authentic confidence is the only way to manifest lasting success and personal and professional relationships.

So, get rid of the concept of: "I need to look like I'm confident, and so I should imitate people who are famous for being confident."

Stop *shoulding* yourself! Embrace your uniqueness and make it shine as never before!

What really works is being *you*. Be kind to yourself and make peace with yourself. Accept who you are and embody your truth. This is the natural and authentic confidence – the only way to get rid of the energy of desperation.

So stop chasing validation, approval, and success. Yes, the feeling of significance can help you feel better, but it will be very short-term. You tell yourself that the more you do something, whether it's getting more followers, more readers, more bestselling book badges, more high-ticket clients, or more appreciation from your boss or family – the more you will love yourself.

However, what can happen is that when you get to your goal, you will not feel happy. Instead, you will want more followers, bestselling badges, or appreciation.

The fantasies of the mind love fake and fleeting feelings of significance. However, from my experience, the best fantasy is the one you create through your heart, right here and right now. You can choose to love yourself and feel validated and appreciated right here, right now.

There is nothing wrong with desiring to manifest success, money, or moving up your career ladder. But before you begin, release the need to control everyone and everything around you.

Simultaneously, if your current desires are centered around manifesting love and extraordinary relationships because you are not feeling love from within you and want others to love you first, you need to be careful not to activate the Law of Repulsion.

Whatever your manifestation goal is, promise yourself right here and right now that you already embody it and feel absolutely at peace with it. Validate and approve yourself- all you need is a simple decision and mindset shift. Feel abundant with feelings of love, positivity, and harmony, and you will become a magnet for people, circumstances, and energies that want to help you on your journey.

Exercise:

Have a look at your previous goals and accomplishments. What was your why? Did you desire significance, approval, and validation?

Was it hard to manifest your desires?

How did others respond to your energy?

What about your current goals and manifestations? Can you already feel whole and complete? Can you embody the energy of love, harmony, peace, and positivity right here and right now?

Important – don't judge yourself when doing this exercise. It's all about learning! We all catch ourselves, "making mistakes" every now and then. But this is how we learn. When you realize you can change something in your way of thinking and acting, be grateful because you are your best teacher. Now you know what not to do, which is a significant step to move forward!

Secret #2 Trying to Re-Program Your Subconscious Mind? Discover Why It Might NOT Work Unless You De-Program It First

Do you know how to make your subconscious mind listen to you? Can you actually imprint your authentic desires and use the power of your subconscious mind to guide you?

Or do you tend to fall back to your old patterns?

We all want something, but, in most cases, we were programmed and conditioned to get something different. At the same time, wanting something is not very helpful because you send a message to the Universe that you don't have it.

The challenge is how to get to the right place of *being* and stop fighting with ourselves. The biggest battle is the one we experience within ourselves as we keep on *wanting* while experiencing inner resistance amplified by rejection from the world.

This section might be a bit difficult to comprehend, especially if you're new to the subconscious or

Secret #2

unconscious mind concepts, so if needed, read it several times. As Bob Proctor says, it's all about repetition. And he's well known for reading the same book - *Think and Grow Rich* every day.

OK, so let's make your subconscious mind work for you! It doesn't have to be hard. You just need to understand the basics.

When you are presented with a new idea, it's just an idea because there is no proof, whether such an idea feels good or bad, empowering or dangerous.

But when you start creating any proof around it, based on your experiences, observations, past hurts, or successes, it becomes a belief, which can be negative or positive. In other words, your belief can be limiting or empowering.

For example, you start a YouTube channel, and it's not growing as fast as you imagined. You research other people's channels, and you say to yourself: *Oh, they have more followers, they are more successful. I will never be like them.*

Of course, for some reason, you don't focus on the fact that other channels have been in the game for many,

many years, and they all started exactly the way you did, if not less successful!

Then some troll posts a negative comment on your videos, and you form a belief that your channel sucks. You are sure it's because of your ethnicity, lack of college degree, or something else such as your hair, teeth, or accent.

Then, your thought is backed up by a negative feeling, and now you are very successfully *not* manifesting your desires. I will add this- as humans, we are real experts in creating negative beliefs. We are successfully creating what we don't want while moving away from our goals.

But this is where the true empowerment can take place (if you allow it!). This is the real secret behind the secret!

You are not broken. There is nothing wrong with you. You are a successful manifestor, no matter what results you get from your efforts. You are already very talented at creating firm beliefs by combining your thoughts with certain feelings. Your mind and body know how to manifest.

For me, this was the most significant *aha* moment on my self-improvement journey. I asked myself- *what if I could positively use my natural powers? What if I used*

Secret #2

my senses, energies, thoughts, and feelings, in a way that is positive and aligns with my goals?

So, let me repeat, whatever "bad results" you have manifested in your life so far, give yourself some credit because you are just very talented at using your mind to create your reality. You can manifest! So now, get excited because you can use the exact same system you have been using your entire life but in a consciously positive and empowering way.

Oh, there will be some side effects to this, so please be warned! One of them is that you will feel more energized. Yes, you will have more energy to do what you love. It will be natural energy. You will no longer need to rely on coffee to get going.

No, I'm not going mad. What you'are reading right here and right now is one of the biggest secrets to manifestation, lifestyle design, or reality creation. Whatever you want to call it.

OK, so you realize you are not broken, and nothing is wrong with you. You know you have been negatively using your inner manifestation system. Perhaps you even got addicted to your old story? Feeling like there is something wrong with you, some heavy dark energies made a pact to get you!

But now, you are making a conscious effort to use your inner manifestation system in a way that aligns with your desires. You realize you were addicted to worrying, stress, and criticism. You decide to quit negativity and gradually start experiencing more energy.

But what happens then? Your subconscious mind was programmed for the negative for so many years. And now, you have more energy to do the things you love. All the time and energy you save on stress, worry, anger, or replaying some gloomy scenes from the past...what are you going to do with this time and energy?

This is when many people self-sabotage and get back to old patterns.

Hey, let's call this old buddy and gossip. Let's scroll on social media and worry we are not good enough. Yes, I know, I know. I was supposed to start my own inspirational Instagram page. And I feel like I could, with all this free time and energy. But...I'm still addicted to my old, negative patterns!

Once again, this is a great talent and skill. So, if you've ever experienced any forms of self-sabotage before, once again, give yourself some credit. You are very good at this. And as a recovering *self-sabotage-holic* (I was the queen of *self-sabotage-holism*, probably one of the most talented ever!) I definitely applaud you!

And once again, It's not my intention to make you feel bad or scared. I want you to feel relaxed and playful, knowing that your inner manifestation system works, and it works very well!

Now you also know the side effects of changing your inner patterns and habits. You might experience more time and energy, and your subconscious mind might start rebelling, saying: "Hey, what are we going to do with all this extra time and energy?"

Once again, as one of the most skilled manifestation experts on this planet, you need to make a choice. Changing your subconscious mind by choosing different thoughts, feelings, and actions may feel uncomfortable.

It's like trying to go on a healthy diet. When you first get started, you feel very tempted to reverse back to your old patterns. Your subconscious mind is just waiting to demonstrate the superiority of your old negative eating patterns and programs.

Secret #2

But you can always choose and start a nice, peaceful dialog with your subconscious mind, using this template:

I used to believe that my old limiting belief was true.

And I thank you, my deep inner mind (or my subconscious mind), for holding on to this belief. Thank you, thank you, thank you. It was so much fun back then.

But NOW, I choose a new belief because I'm a new person.

Use this template as an exercise to start a dialog with your subconscious mind.

But please be warned, you might also be tempted to use your well-deserved title of being the world's leading expert of self-sabotage and negative thoughts. So, what do you choose?

Can you start associating positive thoughts, feelings, and actions with fun? Will you take the challenge of becoming the world's leading expert in the field of positive thinking and acting? Or perhaps you still hold onto your old self-image of negativity, feeling so addicted to it. I mean, you worked very hard. You put so much effort into creating long-lasting negative patterns and habits. You designed a very smart diet for your mind; a diet of stress, worry, anger, sadness. You were extremely successful with this diet for so many years. You stuck with it, without any cheat days! Well done!

And now what? Something new? Changing your mind? Losing your well-deserved achievement of becoming an expert in the field of worry and creating negative movies in your mind?

If you're laughing while reading this- keep laughing because it puts you in a higher vibration and energized state of being. I don't know about you, but I prefer laughter to self-guilt or self-blame. I've been there as well. I will brag about my "credentials" again; I used to be a Self-Guilt Queen. In fact, I was one of the world's leading specialists in the field of self-blame, and I took my title very seriously, always looking for new ways to torture myself with what "I did wrong and what I should have done instead".

If you are not laughing, then no worries, I understand that not everyone gets my sense of humor, and we will get very serious in just a minute!

I see these patterns all the time amongst people who study self-development. They learn a new concept or technique and discover something about themselves. And, very often, their mind starts playing tricks on them, such as: "Oh my God. Look at you! What have you done? You're such a fool. You were doing it all wrong until now! Why didn't you learn about it earlier? Imagine how your life would be different if you had only studied this book earlier. You wasted so many years! And now, look at you!"

The secrets of the world's leading self-guilt trip authorities might be the next book in the series!

But really, stop being so serious and stop *shoulding* yourself. Whenever I get a negative thought or catch myself re-playing some cynical movie from the past or even an imaginary movie of what can go wrong, I just say to myself: "Come on, Elena, this was your old job. In that job, you were an expert on worry, doubts, and fear. But now you're working a different job, remember? Well, it's kind of the same job, but a different department. So yea, keep playing movies, but make them nice and be kind to yourself. Remember? You can be the world's leading expert of positive thinking!"

This is the moment when you get out of your self-imposed negative trance and allow yourself to wake up! Now you can make a conscious decision to use your inner

Secret #2

talents of creating thoughts and emotions to empower and motivate you, rather than get you off track and make you feel unworthy.

Whenever you get a thought and strong emotions are there, you make it into a firm belief (positive and negative). Then, you start looking for proof to confirm your new belief and align it with your insecurities.

Example:

-Oh, I can't be successful because I am a woman

-I don't have money to invest in marketing

-I can't be a motivational speaker because of my accent

-I can't do this, because nobody in my town is doing it

Then, most people feel pain and resistance and try affirmations such as: "I am rich, successful, confident," but from a lack and negativity. Their state of being is very contracted. They might feel angry or frustrated and start reciting some affirmations while hoping for the best.

While these techniques can work, they are just techniques. You try to work hard to change what you believe, or in other words, you can try to re-program yourself by adding some positive techniques while still in a negative state. My personal opinion is that it's always better than not doing anything at all and just complaining.

But what's more useful is embracing the principle of de-programming yourself first! Remember that any technique such as affirmation is just an extension of a timeless manifestation principles rooted in your self-image. In my books, I always underline the concept of fully understanding and integrating the manifestation principles first, such as permanently shifting your mindset and energy. Living by timeless manifestation principles such as what is share in this book, will give you much better results than merely chasing the latest manifestation "hack", without ever attempting to go deeper and working on your mindset and energy.

I don't know about you, but I like results. I don't like trying something half-heartedly while hoping for the best. I like to have a holistic system I can repeatedly use to get better results and keep manifesting the new levels of whatever reality I desire to create for myself.

Before infusing yourself with genuine positivity, you need to face your inner demons and release them. It's like the peeling for the mind and soul. Imagine you want to get some new furniture. Well, first, you will probably get rid of the old one, right? Unless you want to end up in a crammed apartment.

Yet, so many people love cramming their minds with whatever new hack they can find about LOA. And yes, whatever they do, they are very good at it.

Extremely talented Mind Cramming experts! Give them some credit!

You feel bad? Just recite a random affirmation. Stay crammed and confused. *Maybe this will work. I don't know. I just hope. Whatever the wind is, I will fly there.*

You can try hard to change what you believe. But you can also destroy a belief and step into a new one while using your mind to create evidence that it will work for you.

Remember a person who wanted to start a YouTube channel? They worked very hard to find the evidence they couldn't do it. They did their research that confirmed other content creators were successful and had a ton of subscribers.

Well, but how about researching their humble beginnings? Or how about creating a list stating the reasons why you can be successful? Or focusing on your audience and serving it the best you can by creating new

Secret #2

content? How about using your extraordinary talent and expertise to play movies in your mind, but in a more empowering way, while truly feeling your success and acting as if you were successful (because you already are! Remember there is no need to prove anything).

If you enter such an empowered state of being, you will create and upload your videos like crazy.

While this is just an example, whatever you do, you can create positive proof and evidence to make your inner manifestation system work for you, not against you.

I'm using this methodology to keep writing new books! In fact, I've been using my inner system for years. However, at first, I was in my old identity as an international expert on worry, and limiting beliefs. So, I would write a book and feel scared. The movie I kept playing in my mind was extremely negative. In fact, I won several well-acclaimed awards because of my abilities to create negative movies in my mind. I felt anxious and even buried my dreams for a while. Oh, boy, was I good at making those movies back then. But now, when I talk about it, it just seems funny.

For those of you superstitious manifestors who fear that the mere fact of mentioning your old negative patterns will make them manifest and doom you for life, please relax!

Yes, I love positivity, but I'm no fan of toxic positivity. I don't subscribe to burning your head in the sand, pretending it's always so good. No, my friend, you need to be proactive. Face your negative thoughts, be aware of them. Realize they are blocking you on many levels, and make a decision to erase them. Get rid of the old tape, disk, or program and then create a new one. And yes, you will still remember the old negative one, but it will no longer affect you. It will seem a bit unreal, funny, or even grotesque.

Doing affirmations or any other technique is not effective at all if done from a place of resistance.

Doing and being are two different states. It's not that much about what you do. It's about who you are or who you become. What is the intention that you have? Are you doing affirmations from a place of resistance? Whatever you tell yourself (while in a position of resistance, need, and stress) affirms what you don't have.

First, be in a relaxed state. Any state of relaxation helps erase resistance while making your subconscious mind prone to new, empowering suggestions.

Secret #2

The real question is: why do you want to manifest success? To move towards something that excites you, or to get far away from what you hate? The second option automatically implies that your focus is still on what you don't want, which may activate some old, negative programs.

You need to take meaningful and aligned action from a place of emptiness and relaxation. By entering a relaxed state of being, you are no longer aligned with old programs and energies that are holding you back. In other words- you de-program yourself before allowing any new programs in.

Let's say a person who is a business owner is feeling frustrated because they are not attracting enough clients. And suddenly one of their long-term clients decides to ask for a refund! Needless to say, the business owner feels very angry and sad. They keep thinking: *"why does this always happen to me? I work so hard! How could they do this to me?"*

And then, they try to recite several affirmations, such as:

"Oh, but I'm rich, my clients love me."

Which makes them feel even worse because they can feel a massive gap between where they are now and where

Secret #2

they want to be. There's a big split between what they affirm and how they actually feel, think, and act.

What they could do instead is to relax for a few minutes (a few deep breaths can really do the trick) and then write down why they feel grateful for the client who just asked for a refund.

For example: *even though they decided to stop using our services, we really enjoyed working together for many years, and now at least I know the type of clients I want to work with. Maybe, I can ask them for honest feedback as to why they decided to stop using our services and use it to improve my business?*

Such a mental and energetic switch can take place in less than 5 minutes. Then, your mind will start looking for more positive things about this seemingly "negative" situation. And yes, after you've pressed that positivity button in your deep inner mind, you can start using your affirmations or visualizations. You can visualize your bank account or emails from happy clients. You can affirm: *I'm on my way, I'm in the process of transforming my business, I love it, it's so much fun!*

Whatever affirmations (or visualizations) you use, confirm them every day by staying focused on your progress and deep gratitude for everyone and everything around you.

For example, a business owner may feel frustrated because they didn't reach enough clients. At the same time, they can choose to feel grateful for the clients that already enrolled in their programs. They can keep affirming: *"if one person got interested in my services, I'm sure that soon I will have tens, hundreds, or even thousands of interested prospects and clients. I'm on my way!"*

Instead of thinking: *Oh, this will not work, I just suck.* While mindlessly affirming: *I'm a millionaire!*

You want to manifest a healthy body and weight loss? Your original goal was to lose 10 pounds. And you lost 2 pounds. Well, you can choose to complain about the fact that it's taking too long and you still have 8 pounds to lose, and it will probably never work for you anyway because of your genetics, your job, or your spouse. Or you can focus on the fact that you've already lost 2 pounds, and your body knows exactly how much time it needs to lose weight effectively and permanently. For now, why not enjoy the process of learning more about healthy living while using it as an opportunity to transform your life?

Secret #2

Why focus on what is not working? You can focus on what is working- this is the best affirmation and one of the most vital signals you can send to the Universe.

Be your affirmations.

Also, affirmations are not only about what you say. They are also about what you do and what you decide to embody as you go through your daily activities.

The biggest mistake that I see people in the LOA community make is focusing on some new method or technique without genuinely understanding its basic principles.

They may know many different manifestation methods, but since they don't fully understand the principles, they are just paying lip service while mindlessly reciting some affirmations. Maybe it will work, perhaps not. Who knows?

I don't know about you, but I want results.

Whatever it is that you do, always strive to differentiate between timeless principles and on-and-off tactics. For example, many online entrepreneurs get lost in a zillion of tactics such as: *shall I do a podcast, or run Facebook ads, or write blogs?* In reality, all these marketing techniques can work, but the main principle is- is there a market for what you do? Can you communicate your value? And who do you want to attract?

A person who wants to lose weight and live a healthy lifestyle can also get lost in zillions of different diets and meal plans. And they can all be helpful, but people must first embrace the basic principles: *treat your body like a temple and nourish it with real, nutritious food. Move your body, burn some calories, feel energized!*

If you have tried manifesting before using a zillion of tactics, it's time to explore your inner state. I'm pretty sure you already understand the importance of focusing on the positive. I'm all for positivity. But, getting rid of negativity is also essential. You can have the best affirmations in the world, but you will only amplify negativity and magnify what you don't have if you use them while in a negative state.

Consciously train your mind to affirm your little wins as much as you can! Someone smiles at you? Wow, it's because your energy is improving! Have you just made your first sale in your business? Well, it's just the beginning! What about that job interview? Perfect! You're in the right vibration already!

Secret #2

One of the best affirmations you can embrace is looking for confirmations and positive evidence. Give yourself more credit because you are already manifesting your dreams! It's only getting better and better.

Even if something doesn't go your way, you can choose to use it to your advantage. Maybe the Universe wants to test you?

Remember that you can't get rejected. You can only get re-directed. Everything is unfolding just like it should!

Exercise

1. What is your goal or desire you wish to manifest?

Describe all the details using the present tense, as if you already had it.

2. Enter a relaxed and fun state by listening to your favorite song, dancing around, and taking a few deep breaths.

3. Now, have a look at your current reality and everyday activities. What signals are you getting from the Universe? Train your mind to look for as many positive confirmations as you possibly can.

4. When you wake up and go to bed, talk to yourself kindly and keep reminding yourself of all the beautiful things you are already receiving and why you are more than worthy of manifesting all your desires.

Let's say you want to "program yourself" to be a full-time entrepreneur, and this week you had a potential client reaching out to you. Whenever a client reaches out to you for your services, this actually signals your progress! Make sure you appreciate that and give yourself a well-deserved pat on the back.

"Everything is unfolding just like it should; I'm moving forward."

What you're actually doing is crossing the threshold from an opinion to a firm, positive belief because when you show yourself confirmation, your RAS (Reticular Activating System) filters out for things that actually lead to your goal.

So, start to notice more of what is working fine and, if needed, address what is not working from a positive standpoint to improve yourself. You don't fail. You succeed, or you learn!

Secret #3 The Missing Links between Desire and Aligned Action (and the Best Manifestation Shortcut)

As we have already stated: Non-neediness is one of the primary keys to successful and truly happy manifestations.

Yes, you want embody your deep inner faith that you will be successful because you already are successful.

Always remember that your success doesn't need to rely on some external factor. You are already successful. You have already manifested many amazing things, no matter what you have or don't have!

Your mind is continuously making evaluations by asking questions, and it's up to you to make it work in your favor.

One of the biggest lessons I've learned from Tony Robbins is that if we change and empower our questions, we make better and more empowering decisions and choices. In other words- when you change the way you see the world, you change the world.

Secret #3

Now, here's some good news...everybody can manifest and use their mind to create their reality. Whether they are getting the results they actually want is a different story. Most people never wake up, and therefore don't even attempt to take full ownership of their minds.

They set a goal and have a little bit of faith in it in the beginning. But then, they allow some negative thoughts and beliefs to take over. Instead of focusing on what could go well, they focus on what could go wrong. In alignment with their negative thoughts, they take negative actions and never manifest their true desires.

The way it works is best described by Napoleon Hill's Triangle of *Desire-Faith-Action*. To manifest successfully, you need a positive desire backed up with positive faith and action. So many people never get to manifest their desires because they don't take consistent positive action. And the reason why they don't take positive action is that they begin doubting themselves, which leads to losing faith. They start doubting because they don't use their mind to ask empowering positive questions. These questions are the missing link in the desire-faith-and-action triangle.

While some might say that empowering questions are only needed to create faith and that faith automatically leads to action, I'd venture to say that we need empowering questions all the time because they also lead to empowering actions.

There are many ways to create empowering questions that fully support your manifestation journey. However, my favorite method to develop as many empowering questions as you need to is through Identity Shifting.

First, you need to come up with an exciting vision for your life. What do you desire to manifest? And who are you in that vision? What are your thoughts, feelings, and actions? This is the New You or the 2.0 version of You.

To come up with some genuinely empowering questions, start thinking just like your new 2.0 version does.

I used to feel stuck in my desire to become a writer. But I could never take consistent actions to support my vision. I was more like a wannabee, haha. And so, years would pass, I would keep myself busy with other "goals," and I simply wasn't consistent with writing new books.

So, I created a new vision for my life. I said to myself: *"OK, Elena, you are a super creative writer. You are a serial author. You are a writing machine."*

Secret #3

I even visualized my readers visiting me at my home and literally requesting me to write more.

They would even make me tea and coffee and cook my meals. It was a funny, grotesque vision, and it worked very well for me. It's up to you if you decide to use humor in your visualizations.

I also imagined I had deadlines and that instead of being self-employed, I was hired by some secret love-based mindset agents. In that vision, my only job was to write as much as possible because it was a part of the Positivity Mission I was on with other secret agents.

So, I began asking myself empowering questions: *how would my new 2.0 version think? What questions would they ask?*

My old self was in a negative mindset, asking negative questions such as:

-why can't I grow my audience? I guess I will never be successful.

-why can other authors write so fast and I can't? I guess I should just quit before I make a fool out of myself.

-what if some of my friends and family find my work and don't like it? Because you know, I still remember

when I wrote my first poem as a teen, and they just laughed at it.

However, my new self knows how to ask empowering questions such as:

-I wonder how it would feel to get emails from happy readers who appreciate my work?

-Can I write a book to help at least 1 person manifest their desires? And what if I could help 10, 100, or even 1000 people? I mean, other authors can do it. So let's keep writing!

-If I had a mailing list of readers, what kind of emails would I send? Would I share some personal stories? Would I ask for feedback? Would they feel excited to get some excerpts from my new books?

Trust me, it works every time. Whenever you use your mind to create empowering questions, your faith goes to the next level, and you take positive action that feels so aligned that you no longer feel like you "have to motivate and discipline yourself to work harder." You simply embody your desire, faith, and goals by already *being* the person who manifests effortlessly.

Secret #3

Exercise

I strongly recommend you take a little break from reading this book and grab yourself a nice cup of coffee or tea. Relax and write down (in detail):

-Your dream reality (from the first person).

For example:

I am a high-end coach. I'm so excited to be working with all those celebrities, actors, entrepreneurs, and even other coaches. It's such a privilege to help them transform their mindsets to do better in their careers while providing entertainment and transformation to other people. I love my mission!

-Your new, empowering questions (that your new, 2.0 version asks), for example:

What would it feel like to do my own seminars? How would I feel when talking in front of hundreds of people?

Instead of: *why can't I grow my YouTube audience? I guess nobody is interested in what I do. Let's watch Netflix instead! I feel so stupid. Who do I think I was? I could never become a high-end coach. I mean, why would those famous people want to hire me anyway?*

Secret #3

Please note, sometimes a question may seem a bit negative but can be used for positive or growth purposes.

For example, you can ask yourself:

Why can't I grow my YouTube audience? – but from a place of curiosity and playfulness.

Imagine you are a LOA detective on a mission to solve a case! You're like Sherlock Holmes of Manifestation.

Hmmm...let's see. Perhaps it's because you are not uploading enough videos? Or maybe the titles don't resonate with your audience? Or perhaps you could do better thumbnails? Or perhaps it would be a good idea to work with a coach who could improve your communication skills? Or perhaps it's keyword optimization? Or your camera and lightning or audio quality?

Whatever the reason is, there is no place for negativity here because we are solving a very important case while having fun and learning.

Another great (and extremely vibration-raising) exercise you can do is imagine you've already manifested your goal. Let's stick to our previous example of a high-end coach.

Secret #3

So now, you are giving a speech at some incredible, high-vibe seminar. You can see all your role models and mentors sitting in the audience, listening to your story while nodding and smiling. Many find your speech inspiring and breathtaking.

In that speech, you share what it took to be successful and all the obstacles you had to overcome, and how grateful you feel for them now because they made you who you are today!

And remember, you are always in control. We all get bombarded with negative thoughts because our brain has only one goal. It wants to keep us safe. I, too, get negative thoughts such as:

Oh, what if someone doesn't like my work?

Then, I catch myself getting off track and immediately say to myself: "*cancel-cancel- cancel.*" I immediately ask myself:

Hmm, what if I publish this book and people like it? What if they post a positive review? And, it's not even about reviews. What if they actually apply my techniques, use them to transform their lives, and then start helping other people too?

Secret #3

Both positivity and negativity are infectious. The levels of effort required to spread negativity are the same as the efforts needed to spread positivity. It's just a question of getting used to embodying positivity and making it your lifestyle. Embodying positivity while looking for confirmations of what is already working in your favor is the best affirmation (and visualization) you could create! Stay focused on the process.

So why not choose positivity and make it your default state?

If you're looking for an actual method to apply after reading this book, then be sure to use empowering questions and start writing them down. Be consistent, do it every day. Even one empowering question a day can be a missing piece to your manifestation journey and can really supercharge your efforts!

You can also combine empowering questions with gratitude. First, write down a few things you are grateful for right now in your current reality to really get in a good vibe. Then, write down a few things you are thankful for. Things that you know already exist in your new reality (in other words, something you haven't manifested yet, but are already grateful for). Finally, write down at least one empowering question.

Secret #3

Don't get stuck where so many people do. You need positive desire, faith, and action – and the best way to consistently keep fueling all three is with empowering questions!

Secret #4 Manifest Faster By Slowing Down! (The #1 Thing to Learn from Mindful Manifestors)

Some days you may start experiencing impatience. *Why is it taking so long? What can I do to manifest faster? Maybe I need to get a new manifestation skill? Or perhaps this method isn't for me?*

It's absolutely normal to start experiencing impatience every now and then. I've been there too! And what I've learned is that whenever you feel impatient, you have two choices. You can push harder and start obsessing about your goals, while experiencing anxiety.

Or, you can use your impatience as a signal from the Universe that you need to relax and let go a bit! Trust me when I say this- the second option works much better!

As an impatient manifestor, you may feel tempted to end up with the first option while turning your impatience into anxiety and unhealthy obsession.

But, in nature, everything needs time. And you need to let go and relax. Be grateful that your mind is sending

Secret #4

you all those amazing signals through the feelings of impatience, and schedule some time for self-care to allow your mind to stop focusing on your goals so that it can relax and rejuvenate. My favorite way of doing so is by incorporating simple mindfulness techniques into my life.

You can enjoy the moment and allow yourself to let go of small, gradual changes in life, even if you're busy. Mindfulness doesn't have to be complicated. It's not about levitating over your bed; it's about tuning in with your senses. Embracing a mindful lifestyle will allow you to concentrate and work better while enjoying all the little things in your life and reducing anxious states.

"To let go means to give up coercing, resisting, or struggling, in exchange for something more powerful and wholesome which comes out of allowing things to be as they are without getting caught up in your attraction to or rejection of them, in the intrinsic stickiness of wanting, of liking and disliking. Just watch this moment without trying to change it at all. What is happening? What do you feel? What do you see? What do you hear?" - by Jon Kabat-Zinn

Mindfulness Meditation is all about perceiving, concentrating, observing, and cultivating the present moment. It's one of the best ways to enter a relaxed state while raising your vibration! Below are my favorite mindfulness techniques- feel free to choose the ones you like and start practicing them to erase impatient and anxious states. After all, you don't want to be a stressed-out manifestor. Instead, you want to experience peace, happiness, and relaxation while sending out a positive vibration to the Universe- you feel calm knowing everything is unfolding just like it should, and you choose to enjoy the present moment.

Mindful Anchor Exercise

Keep your attention focused on any object of your choice for a few minutes or more. It can be a statue, a picture, a tree, a flower, or a candle. Set the alarm to give yourself a few minutes of peace.

Fall in Love with Breathing

Breathe in and out several times. Find out where you feel your breath – is it your chest, stomach, rib cage, nose, mouth, or throat? What happens, and what sensations do you experience after changing the duration of your breath (making it longer or shorter)? Don't judge yourself. Whatever it is, let it be and embrace curiosity. This will allow you to tune into your body and mind and read whatever signal you get from them quickly and effortlessly!

Ice cube meditation.

To do this mindfulness exercise, simply hold an ice cube in your hand until it melts. Let the melted ice spill onto your lap or on the table. Observe your sensations and feelings. Do you feel discomfort? Do you feel like quitting? Mindfully register whatever happens in your body.

Digital detox

When do you usually feel tempted to check your phone? What are your emotional triggers that make you scroll on social media or check your email? Is it really necessary? Analyze if you do it before you get out of bed, during meals, while talking to someone else, maybe on the bus? Allow yourself to spend a day without your phone. Plan ahead by writing down all the impulses that make you check your phone. Is it sadness? Impatience? Boredom? What if, instead of checking your phone, you could meditate or do a simple mindfulness exercise, or go for a short walk?

Curious Walking

Go on a mindful walk. It can be in your local park or any open space in nature. Explore the place without any purpose. Begin by feeling the sensation of your feet stepping on and off the ground. Allow your mind to register everything you see and feel. When your thoughts drift in a different direction, try to get your attention back on your feet, as well as the air you breathe and the sounds you hear.

Mindful Tea or Coffe Break

Make yourself a cup of your favorite tea or coffee. Breathe in the scent. Savor the flavor. Feel the temperature and mindfully enjoy it!

Whenever your mind drifts, and you catch yourself stressing out about your everyday concerns, pay attention to different parts of your body: your feet, ankles, legs, hips, hands, etc. Feel how you fill your lungs with air and imagine that you bring that breath to every part of your body. Then, carry on sipping your tea or coffee! If you don't have the time to meditate for hours, you can choose to turn your tea or coffee breaks into mini mindfulness meditations while letting go of stress, worry, and impatience.

Simple Seated Meditation

Sit down in a comfortable position. Put your hands on your knees, palms down, or put one hand on the other. Imagine that your head is a helium balloon. Let it rise naturally and stretch your spine. Lean back and forth a few times until you find the midpoint of balance.

Focus on your breathing. Make sure your mind doesn't wander. If you notice that you have lost concentration, come back. No judgment here!

Simple Sound Meditation

Start by noticing the sounds in your body, the sounds in the room you are in, the sounds in the building, and finally, the sounds outside. Let the sounds sink in instead of struggling to capture them. Listen mindfully. Keep it up for about ten more minutes.

When you are ready, draw attention from outside sounds to your thoughts. Watch how thoughts arise and go. As soon as you notice that your attention becomes entangled in a thread of ideas, take a step back calmly, away from

Secret #4

your thoughts, and return to observe them in the distance, as much as you can.

As you can see, mindfulness is a lifestyle choice, and it doesn't have to be about long or complicated rituals. It's all about understanding how to observe whatever happens around and inside you. Become an observer of your reality and take joy in being able to be a part of it.

Promise yourself to appreciate the present moment and feel good about it because it's thanks to living and fully being in the present moment that you can let go of past hurts and mindfully create a fantastic future.

Secret#5 Does Your Environment Block Your Manifestations? (Feng Shui It Up to Show the Universe You are Ready to Receive!)

Have a closer look at your home and office. Does your environment affirm your desires?

For example, if your workspace is cluttered, you may find yourself feeling stuck in your professional life, not manifesting your career goals successfully.

If you want to attract more money and abundance into your life, does your wallet reflect your desires? For example, if your wallet is old and full of clutter, such as some old receipts, no wonder it's getting harder and harder to manifest more money into your life.

What about your handbag, purse, backpack or car? Are they too filled with objects you no longer need? What about those old papers and receipts?

Do you often find yourself holding onto clutter and old stuff? *Because maybe one day, you will need them.*

Secret #5

Well, have a closer look at your wardrobe. How would you feel about getting rid of your old clothes? How much of old energy is actually accumulating in your personal objects and surroundings? Does the new, 2.0 version of you actually need all this old stuff? Wouldn't it be better to at least do some serious decluttering and release all the old energy while making space for the new?

It's time to have a look at a few timeless Feng Shui tips to make sure you fully affirm your desires while attracting new, empowering energies. Many people worldwide are successfully using these principles to manifest happiness, health, prosperity, and freedom.

The Feng Shui practice focuses on the energy that moves in and around our home and all its rooms. While detailed Feng Shui practices require hiring a professional Feng Shui consultant, the basic principles are easy to understand and apply. They are also very intuitive, some would even say – common sense!

Like in the traditional Chinese medicine, where *chi* is said to flow through the body, in Feng Shui, the *chi*, also called vital force, is thought to flow through our homes.

Clutter is the number one thing you want to get rid of because air and energy elements must always be in motion. And clutter traps all positive energy and keeps us stuck in the past. When I say clutter, I refer to old papers, old books, old clothes, old gadgets, as well as digital clutter, for example, old files on your computer.

Believe it or not, last year, I felt very stuck on my writing journey. So, I decided to declutter my house, paying closer attention to my office and my computer. I immediately felt more energized and creative! I also realized that I was desperately hanging onto some old ideas that originated from my old self and were no longer aligned with my new vision.

I felt scared to get rid of some of my old files because, I thought, maybe one day, I could turn them into bestselling books! I spent a couple of years in this funk. Holding on to several "unfinished manuscripts" that consisted of a few random pages each.

So, whatever it is you're feeling stuck with at the moment, it's time you scheduled some decluttering as soon as possible.

Here are a few more tips:

1. Get rid of all broken items, or have them repaired, replace burned out bulbs, donate, or sell, all things that you have not used in the last 8 months. Let other people enjoy what you're no longer enjoying or aren't passionate about. When you have finished cleaning, wash your hands under running water and sea salt for at least one minute.

2. In Feng Shui, the front door of your house means addressing the issue of the "mouth of chi." So it is essential to help bring good energy into your home by keeping it clean and well lit. You need to remove all the clutter from inside your front door, so you don't block out all the good energy. After you're done with your front door, repeat the process with the other doors in your house as well as your windows.

3. Get ready to use some color therapy in conjunction with decluttering and Feng Shui. You can paint your front door green to attract financial abundance. Red color can bring prosperity and romance. Blue attracts awareness and relaxation. At the same time, brown attracts stability. Even those who don't practice Feng Shui know that experimenting with different colors in your home can drastically change your mood. And by

focusing on the activities that put you in a good mood, you automatically manifest more good things into your life.

Plants bring vibrant *chi* into a home or work environment. Home offices require as much good energy as possible, so why not surround ourselves with vibrant and vigorous plants? You can experiment with large plants such as lilies, bamboo, and jade varieties known to be a very high vibe. If you don't have enough space, you can use a smaller plant which is better than nothing. It's essential to keep your plants healthy and well-fed. This can give you a lot of peace and calm. Taking care of your plants is very therapeutic and symbolizes your willingness to invest in yourself and your inner growth.

5.Although most people overlook it, music also plays a significant role in Feng Shui and manifestation. For example, if your home is too quiet, you may create too much *yin* or passive energy. That can affect your mood, making you feel a bit lethargic. So, if you want to manifest higher energy levels, put on some soft music for 10 minutes every day.

6.To attract even more "yang" or good energy, open all your windows when you are cleaning your home. Each room must be ventilated regularly while allowing in some fresh air.

7. Keep all your cleaning equipment in a closet or, if possible, outside your house to block negative energy.

8. A broom even as an ornament for your front door is not recommended since you don't want the positive energy entering your home to be swept away.

9. If your goal is attracting more productivity and creativity, avoid placing your desk in a position directly in front of a window as it can throw all your creativity out. If your goal is to work efficiently, try positioning your desk with the window to one side. So you can look out the window when you need a break without interrupting the flow of creativity.

10. If you want to attract love and romance into your life, have a closer look at your bedroom. Do you sleep in a single or double bed? If you sleep in a double bed, which is your and your partner's side? Are you making space in your home to consciously attract a partner of your dreams? Or does your home scream, "I'm single for life?"

Have a look at your surroundings and start thinking like your new 2.0 version. Create space for new energies and get rid of what is no longer serving you. Mindfully create new habits to keep increasing your quality of life and making your space work for you.

In fact, I highly recommend you start decluttering now! If you're busy, start off with your car, your bag, or your wallet. If your goal is attracting more money and abundance - get a new wallet. Enjoy the feeling of filling it with cash and credit cards!

Also, schedule half an hour of decluttering a day, and start working your way through all your belongings until you're done. If you prefer, you can just go cold turkey and declutter all your belongings in one day.

After getting rid of your clutter and rearranging your space, you will start feeling more peaceful and energized. Help your environment help you! Also, please note, this work never ends. In fact, it should become a habit. I go on regular decluttering sprees several times a year, and it really feels great!

One of the biggest spiritual benefits of decluttering is that you get rid of the resistance of letting go. Old objects you no longer need also represent old mindsets, energies, feelings, and emotions. Ask yourself if you can really afford to hang on to the old? Or are you ready to step up,

Secret #5

embrace your new self and finally release whatever it is that's blocking your new levels of manifesting?

Conclusion – Trust Yourself

Keep expanding and keep moving forward! Remember to use your precious mind as a filter. Filter out any negative beliefs as well as old concepts and paradigms that are blocking your manifestations. Keep analyzing your new self-image while mindfully aligning your thoughts with what you want. Don't get too stuck with the latest manifestation "hack". Instead focus on the timeless principles described in this book.

Remember that you attract who you are. So, keep aligning your thoughts, feelings, and actions with what you want. Watch your energy transform. Embody your desires. Be your desires. Affirm your desires with what you do and how you think about yourself, not only with what you say.

It all starts with your mind and understanding how to take care of it. Knowing how to control what enters or leaves your mind is one of the best skills to develop on your spirituality and self-improvement journey.

Don't get discouraged or impatient if it takes longer to manifest your desires. The journey itself is your destination. As you are exploring yourself and your manifestation abilities, you become a better person. You are kind to yourself and others while cultivating a positive mindset infused with endless gratitude. That alone is a gift to those around you!

Keep practicing what you have learned, and keep sharing these concepts with others. Together we can change the world by collectively enhancing the vibration of the planet.

I genuinely hope that this book inspired you and gave you new tools to expand your consciousness and raise your awareness.

You are limitless, you are powerful, and you are amazing!

I believe in you and wish you all the best on your journey!

If you have a few minutes, I'd really appreciate it if you could leave me a short review on Amazon. Let other LOA readers in our community know who this book can help and why.

Thank You Thank You Thank You,
I hope we "meet" again,
Much love,

Elena

Trust Yourself

For more information and resources about LOA and manifestation, visit my website:

www.LOAforSuccess.com

If you'd like to say hi, please email me at:elena@LOAforSuccess.com

More from Elena G.Rivers

Free LOA Newsletter + Bonus Gift

To help you AMPLIFY what you've learned in this book, I'd like to offer you a free copy of my **LOA Workbook – a powerful, FREE 5-day program (eBook & audio)** designed to help you raise your vibration while eliminating resistance and negativity.

To sign up for free, visit the link below now:

www.loaforsuccess.com/newsletter

More from Elena G. Rivers

You'll also get free access to my highly acclaimed, uplifting **LOA Newsletter.**

Through this email newsletter, I regularly share all you need to know about the manifestation mindset and energy.

My newsletter alone helped hundreds of my readers manifest their own desires.

Plus, whenever I release a new book, you can get it at a deeply discounted price or even for free.

You can also start receiving my new audiobooks published on Audible at no cost!

To sign up for free, visit the link below now:

www.loaforsuccess.com/newsletter

I'd love to connect with you and stay in touch with you while helping you on your LOA journey!

If you happen to have any technical issues with your sign up, please email us at:

support@LOAforSuccess.com

More Books by Elena G. Rivers

Law of Attraction Short Reads Series

Money Mindset: Stop Manifesting What You Don't Want and Shift Your Subconscious Mind into Money & Abundance

How Not to Manifest: Manifestation Mistakes to Avoid and How to Finally Make LOA Work for You

More from Elena G.Rivers

Visualization Demystified: The Untold Secrets to Re-Program Your Subconscious Mind and Manifest Your Dream Reality in 5 Simple Steps

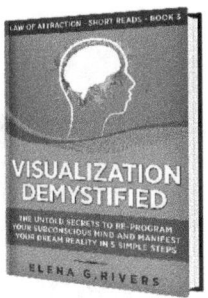

Law of Attr-Action for Entrepreneurs: Advanced Identity Shifting Secrets to Manifest the Income & Impact You Deserve

More from Elena G.Rivers

The Love of Attraction: Tested Secrets to Let Go of Fear-Based Mindsets, Activate LOA Faster, and Start Manifesting Your Desires!

www.ingramcontent.com/pod-product-compliance
Lightning Source LLC
Chambersburg PA
CBHW051831160426
43209CB00006B/1118